WE THE PEOPLE

The California Gold Rush

by Jean F. Blashfield

Content Adviser: Professor Sherry L. Field,
Department of Social Science Education,
College of Education, The University of Georgia

Reading Adviser: Dr. Linda D. Labbo,
Department of Reading Education,
College of Education, The University of Georgia

COMPASS POINT BOOKS
Minneapolis, Minnesota

Compass Point Books
3722 West 50th Street, #115
Minneapolis, MN 55410

Visit Compass Point Bookson the Internet at *www.compasspointbooks.com* or e-mail your request
to *custserv@compasspointbooks.com*

Photography ©: North Wind Picture Archives, cover; Archive Photos, 5 top; North Wind Picture
Archives, 5 bottom; Visuals Unlimited/Stan Skaggs, 6; North Wind Picture Archives, 7; California
Historical Society/North Baker Research Library/FN32019, 8; North Wind Picture Archives, 9;
Visuals Unlimited/Jon Turk, 11; Visuals Unlimited/Link, 12; Archive Photos, 14; Corbis/
Bettmann, 15; Corbis/Museum of Flight, Seattle/PEMCO-Webster & Stevens Collection, 16;
North Wind Picture Archives, 18; Visuals Unlimited, 19; Corbis/Bettmann, 21; North Wind
Picture Archives, 23; Corbis/Hulton-Deutsch Collection, 24; Corbis/Bettmann, 25, 26; North Wind
Picture Archives, 27; Corbis, 29; Corbis/Hulton-Deutsch Collection, 30; Corbis/Carl Corey, 32;
California Historical Society/FN-22860, 34; Corbis/Bettmann, 35; North Wind Picture Archives,
36; Archive Photos/American Stock, 38; Corbis/Bettmann, 41.

Editors: E. Russell Primm and Emily J. Dolbear
Photo Researcher: Svetlana Zhurkina
Photo Selector: Dawn Friedman
Design: Bradfordesign, Inc.
Cartography: XNR Productions, Inc.

Library of Congress Cataloging-in-Publication Data

Blashfield, Jean F.
    The California Gold Rush / by Jean F. Blashfield.
      p. cm. — (We the people)
    Includes bibliographical references and index.
    Summary: Describes adventures and disasters in the lives of people who rushed to the gold
mines of California in 1848 and explains how this event sparked the state's development.
    ISBN 0-7565-0041-9
    1. California—Gold discoveries—Juvenile literature. 2. California—History—1846–1850—
Juvenile literature. 3. Frontier and pioneer life—California—Juvenile literature. [1. California—
Gold discoveries. 2. California—History—1846–1850. 3. Frontier and pioneer life—California.]
I. Title. II. We the people (Compass Point Books).
    F865 .B64 2000
    979.4'03—dc21   00-008670

TABLE OF CONTENTS

Discovering Gold 5

When California Was Spanish 9

Drawn by Gold 15

"Goin' to California, My Banjo on My Knee" ... 18

"Staking a Claim" 20

Life in the Camps 22

The Process of Mining 25

"Mining" the Miners 28

Women of the Gold Rush 33

The Gold Effects 37

The Forty-Niner 40

Glossary 42

Did You Know? 43

Important Dates 44

Important People 45

Want to Know More? 46

Index 48

OREGON COUNTRY

Oregon Trail

California Trail

Oregon Trail

Humboldt R.

Great Salt L.

Great Salt Lake Desert

Hastings Cutoff

Donner Pass

Coloma

American R.

Sacramento

Sonoma

San Francisco

Truckee R.

UTAH TERRITORY

Colorado R.

SIERRA NEVADA

SACRAMENTO VALLEY

Pacific Ocean

CALIFORNIA

NEW MEXICO TERRITORY

N

0   100   200 miles
0   100   200 kilometers

BAJA

MEXICO

Boundaries of 1850
Gold mining area

Map of California Gold Rush

DISCOVERING GOLD

Captain John Sutter was a Swiss settler with a large grant of land in the Sacramento Valley in California. He set out to build an empire of his own, using Indian and Mexican laborers.

John Sutter

James Marshall

In 1848, he hired a carpenter named James Marshall to help build a sawmill at Coloma, on the south fork of the American River. This new sawmill was in fact located 50 miles (80 kilometers) east of Sutter's large tract of land.

The sawmill where Marshall discovered gold

On January 24, 1848, Marshall was testing
the mill wheel. As usual, the water running over
it carried some sand and light gravel. But this time
Marshall saw something sparkling in the sand.
He picked out some small, odd-shaped beads of
yellow metal. Marshall had the camp washer-
woman test the beads in lye, a harsh chemical.

When the beads did not react to the harsh chemical, Marshall knew he had found gold. In an effort to protect his land, Sutter tried to keep the gold a secret.

Sam Brannan

Two weeks later, however, a San Francisco newspaper owner named Sam Brannan spread the word. He loaded up on supplies and set up a business. Then he walked through the streets of the village and shouted, "Gold! Gold!"

Within days, the village was almost a ghost town. Shopkeepers, blacksmiths, and others had left to find gold and instant wealth.

They were the first of about 300,000 people who eventually flocked to the mountains east of San Francisco. Few of them understood how hard life would be there or how few of them would actually find gold.

The California Star *newspaper*

WHEN CALIFORNIA WAS SPANISH

Starting in the 1500s, Spain searched for gold in North America, as it had in South and Central America. When Mexico won its independence from Spain in 1821, Mexico also got Spain's North American colonies.

Spanish fighters in California

In the 1840s, the United States was growing in the East. Thousands of people traveled along the Oregon Trail every month. California, Arizona, and New Mexico still belonged to Mexico, however.

Most Americans in California arrived by ship. They made a long voyage around Cape Horn at the southern tip of South America. Then, in 1844, a group led by a mountain man named Elisha Stevens turned south from the Oregon Trail. They unloaded five wagons and hauled them over a peak in the Sierra Nevada and into the Sacramento Valley. It was the opening of the California Trail.

Some settlers followed Elisha Stevens's route into the Sacramento Valley. The timing of these

Cape Horn

Donner Pass

journeys was very important. One party, led by George and Jacob Donner, started too late in the spring of 1846. By the time they reached the pass through the Sierra Nevada, it was snowing. They were snowbound. The party of eighty-two travelers built makeshift shelters to keep from freezing, but they ran out of food. Only forty-seven people survived. Today, that pass is called Donner Pass.

Despite such bad luck, many American settlers did reach California. Of course, about 10,000 Mexican ranchers and their employees already lived there.

In 1846, the Mexican War broke out between the United States and Mexico. American explorer John C. Frémont encouraged the new

Californians to rebel against Mexico. They raised a flag—the Bear Flag—over the settlement of Sonoma in the Sacramento Valley. That nation, or **republic**, lasted only a few weeks before U.S. soldiers raised the American flag at Monterey and claimed California

John C. Frémont

for the United States. California's state flag still says California Republic.

Mexico lost the war in 1848. It agreed to give the United States all of California except the Baja, a **peninsula** that lies south of California. The Mexicans did not know that gold had already been discovered in California.

DRAWN BY GOLD

After Sam Brannan broke the news about the discovery of gold at Sutter's Mill, most men in San Francisco had gone to the American River to find gold. The news soon spread, and several thousand men from the West came to the Sierra Nevada that year.

Gold miners pose for a group portrait.

15

Crowds bound for California gather at a dock in Seattle, Washington.

By January 1849, fortune hunters had begun to arrive from all over the world, including England, Australia, Peru, and China. Those who arrived that year were called "Forty-Niners"—and were counted in the 1850 U.S. census. Now California had enough residents to become a state. On September 9, 1850, California was admitted to the Union.

In the East, people rarely earned more than a dollar a day. Stories flew that in the goldfields, 1 ounce (31 grams) of gold—no heavier than a stick of gum—would bring fifteen dollars!

Many businessmen gave up their jobs. University students left their classes. Farmers decided to let someone else plow their fields. Soldiers left their posts. Some men took families along, but most went alone.

"GOIN' TO CALIFORNIA, MY BANJO ON MY KNEE"

Stephen Foster's 1848 melody "Oh Susanna" became the theme song of the people heading for California. They went by sea and by land.

By land, it was some 3,000 miles (4,827 km) from the East Coast to California. By sea, it was

Sailing around Cape Horn in South America

A miner travels by ox and wagon.

18,000 miles (28,962 km) from the East Coast sailing south around South America and then north to San Francisco. The voyage took six months, and conditions were terrible.

It cost a lot of money to travel by ship too, so most people traveled by wagon over the Oregon Trail. They joined settlers from Missouri heading for Oregon across the Continental Divide in Wyoming. From there, the gold seekers headed south to cross the Sierra Nevada and enter the Sacramento Valley.

"STAKING A CLAIM"

At the start of the Gold Rush, no laws existed about rights to land on which gold was discovered. The camps made their own rules. Usually a man could claim only as much land along a river as he could dig—sometimes no more than 100 square feet (9 square meters).

To stake a **claim**, a **prospector** pounded wooden stakes into the ground to mark his area. If the claim turned out to have no gold, he would just "pull up stakes" and move on.

In time, there were too many prospectors for the amount of land that might have gold. Soon, newcomers had to buy claims. To trick people into buying land that had no gold, some sellers planted gold on—or "salted"—their claim.

Miners put up wooden stakes such as this one to mark their claims.

LIFE IN THE CAMPS

Gold seekers were more interested in digging for gold than in living well. One gold seeker from Boston, Massachusetts, described setting up a home this way: "I pitched my tent, built a stone chimney at one end, made a mattress of fir [branches], and thought myself well fixed for the winter."

In camps with such names as Lousy Ravine and Whiskey Flat, diggers lived in shacks they built themselves. They used wagons from the Oregon Trail, pieces of lumber, bits of canvas, or anything else they could find. Often the only complete buildings were saloons and dance halls.

Gold seekers arrived without giving any thought to how or what they were going to eat.

The price of food soared, and some men starved rather than leave their claim to get food. Weakened, they couldn't fight off disease and many died.

After a hard day of digging, miners wanted to relax and be entertained. Those who still had

Miners enjoy themselves dancing at the end of a hard day.

money to spend—or had found a few flakes of gold—went to the saloons. They could get a drink, sing, chat with a woman, or tell tales to each other.

Samuel Clemens

One common tale involved a cheating man and a bet made on a frog's ability to jump. In the 1860s, a young writer named Samuel Clemens, who had recently begun to use the name Mark Twain, heard the tale. He turned it into "The Notorious Jumping Frog of Calaveras County," the story that made Mark Twain famous.

THE PROCESS OF MINING

The easiest way to find gold was to **pan** for it. *Panning* means scooping up sand from a riverbed in a pan and swirling it around until the lighter material has poured out. Gold, one of the heaviest materials known, sinks to the bottom.

Those who had no running water on their claim used pickaxes and shovels to dig into the

Panning for gold

25

Miners use long wooden frames called sluices to find gold.

hillsides, looking for gold. Sometimes prospectors built long wooden frames called **sluices**. They poured large quantities of gravel and soil through the frames along with lots of water. Again, the gold sank to the bottom.

Eventually, some prospectors joined forces to create hard-rock mines. These mines followed a layer of quartz, which was often found along with gold, deep into the mountains. A gold vein is also called a **lode**. The Sierra Nevada goldfield was often referred to as the Mother Lode.

In hard-rock mining, the ore had to be hauled out of the ground and crushed in huge machines. These loud machines ran twenty-four hours a day. It was dangerous work.

Underground mines

"MINING" THE MINERS

Very few gold seekers ever found gold. Most of the people who made money in the Gold Rush earned it by selling supplies to the gold seekers. They "mined" the miners.

At the docks or at the end of the trail, **peddlers** tried to sell newcomers digging sites, space in rooming houses, equipment, food, clothing, or information. Some offered newcomers a chance to buy in on a "sure thing."

Many newcomers lasted only a few weeks. Panning and digging were hard, dirty jobs. Discouragement set in easily. Some fell prey to crooks. Others got sick and died. Many diseases were widespread in the makeshift camps. A

Supply tents sold supplies to miners.

Main Street in a Gold Rush town

disease called cholera, spread by dirty water, killed many people. Those who survived often looked for another way to make a living.

The people who sold supplies to the miners built California. They constructed houses, grew food, baked bread, provided entertainment, opened schools and churches—and buried the dead.

One person who made his money supplying the miners was Levi Strauss. A peddler from Germany, he started out selling canvas for tents. Then Strauss hired a seamstress to sew some pants for miners who had to kneel on rock all day. He quickly sold out.

Strauss switched from a canvas fabric to a tough cotton cloth called denim. He dyed the material a deep blue, reinforced the seams of the pants with copper rivets, and called the new pants Levi's. The rest is history.

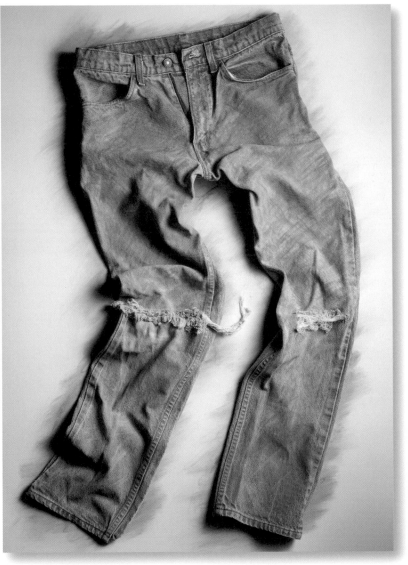

An early pair of Levi's jeans

WOMEN OF THE GOLD RUSH

About 98 percent of the people who were lured west to California with the hopes of great riches during the Gold Rush were men. A few women were entertainers and others worked as saloon keepers. Some even worked in the field camps as cooks and washerwomen.

Part of the attraction for women of the Gold Rush was that they could earn their own money. That was important when Californians wrote their state constitution in 1850. They allowed women to keep their own property and money when they married—a right that was unheard of in the other states.

One of the most famous women of the Gold

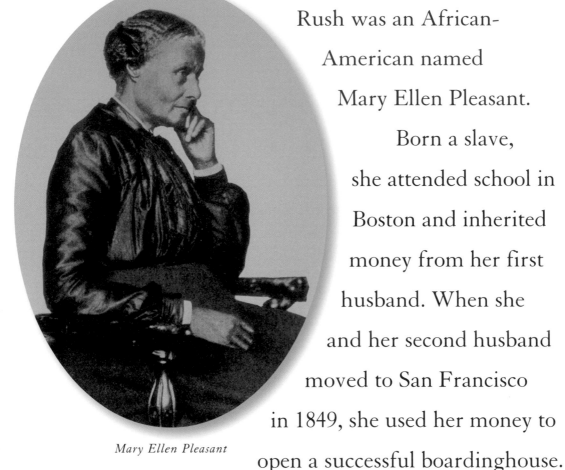

Mary Ellen Pleasant

Rush was an African-American named Mary Ellen Pleasant. Born a slave, she attended school in Boston and inherited money from her first husband. When she and her second husband moved to San Francisco in 1849, she used her money to open a successful boardinghouse. Pleasant may also have lent out money— and gained interest on it. She used her money to help African-Americans in the community. She is known as a founder of civil rights laws in California.

34

Women in the camps helped turn that mass of men and mud into towns. They had well-kept boardinghouses and churches. Schools opened as early as 1850.

Women often ran laundry businesses to wash miners' clothes.

The early days of San Francisco

THE GOLD EFFECTS

Of some 100,000 people who actually went digging for gold, not many found it. And when they did, even fewer managed to hang onto it. But some were lucky. By 1860, more than $500 million in gold—worth about $10 billion today—had been mined!

The biggest effect of the Gold Rush was the new state's exploding population of different nationalities. California became—and continues to be—a place of great diversity.

San Francisco, which began as the Mexican village of Yerba Buena, was many miles away from the gold mines. But it became the central city of the Gold Rush and the entire West.

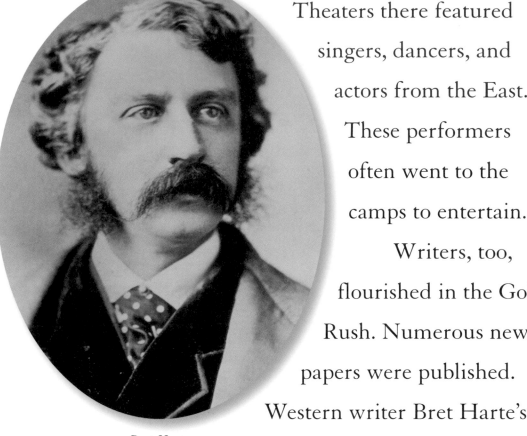

Bret Harte

Theaters there featured singers, dancers, and actors from the East. These performers often went to the camps to entertain. Writers, too, flourished in the Gold Rush. Numerous newspapers were published. Western writer Bret Harte's stories "The Luck of Roaring Camp" and "The Outcasts of Poker Flat" were both set in the Gold Rush.

The effects of the Gold Rush were not always good—especially for Native Americans. Perhaps

90 percent of them had already died of diseases brought by the Spanish. When California became a state, the new constitution put the remaining Native Americans practically into a state of slavery. Miners were allowed to put them to work in the gold mines. Between 1845 and 1870, the number of Indians in California dropped from 150,000 to fewer than 30,000.

The environment also suffered. The rivers were polluted, and the land was churned up, killing all living things. In many places, the devastation caused by the Gold Rush can still be seen.

THE FORTY-NINER

Writer Richard Reinhardt says, "The Forty-Niner, with his recklessness, his youth, his optimism, became the state's defining figure." Many Californians treasure the idea that their state grew from hardy, independent gold seekers. They like to remember that the Forty-Niners settled their state. But at the same time, Californians remember that their settling of the state changed the lives of Native Americans forever.

To this day, Californians are reminded of their Gold Rush heritage. After all, California is now known as the Golden State. The state flower is the golden poppy, and the state's motto is *Eureka!,* meaning "I have found it!"

Forty-Niners helped settle California.

GLOSSARY

claim—a piece of land staked out by the owner

lode—a layer of gold in rock

pan—to sift sand in a pan of water in search of gold

peddlers—people who sell things outside or door-to-door

peninsula—a piece of land nearly surrounded by water

prospector—a person who searches for gold

republic—a nation

sluices—long wooden frames used for catching gold

DID YOU KNOW?

- When James Marshall smashed the small bead of yellow metal between two rocks, it flattened but did not shatter.

- In the earliest days of the Gold Rush, many claims yielded $300 to $400 a day.

- When the economy soared during the California Gold Rush, prices soared too. Eggs cost 50 cents each, boots cost $20 a pair, and potatoes cost $1 a pound (0.4 kg). This was at a time when people rarely earned more than $1 a day!

- The California Gold Rush contributed billions of dollars to the growth of the United States.

IMPORTANT DATES

Timeline

1821	Mexico gains its independence from Spain.
1844	Elisha Stevens and his group turn south from the Oregon Trail and travel over the Sierra Nevada, opening the California Trail.
1846–1848	The United States fights Mexico in the Mexican War.
1848	James Marshall discovers gold at Sutter's Mill on January 24; Mexico loses the war and the United States takes over California on February 2.
1849	The California Gold Rush begins.
1850	California becomes the 31st state in the Union on September 9.

IMPORTANT PEOPLE

JOHN C. FRÉMONT
(1813–1890), *American explorer*

JAMES MARSHALL
(1810–1885), *carpenter who discovered gold at Sutter's Mill in Coloma, California*

MARY ELLEN PLEASANT
(c. 1814–1904), *founder of civil rights laws in California*

LEVI STRAUSS
(1829–1902), *inventor of blue jeans*

CAPTAIN JOHN SUTTER
(1803–1880), *owner of Sutter's Mill*

WANT TO KNOW MORE?

At the Library

Altman, Linda Jacobs. *The California Gold Rush in American History*. Springfield, N.J.: Enslow Publishers, 1997.

Blake, Arthur, and Pamela Dailey. *The Gold Rush of 1849: Staking a Claim in California*. Brookfield, Conn.: Millbrook Press, 1995.

McNeer, May Yonge. *The California Gold Rush*. New York: Random House, 1987.

Van Steenwyk, Elizabeth. *The California Gold Rush: West with the Forty-Niners*. New York: Franklin Watts, 1991.

On the Web

California's Gold Rush Country: Historic Sites and Spectacular Scenery

http://www.goldrush1849.com/

For a brief history of the Gold Rush, including a map and photographs

Gold Rush! California's Untold Stories

http://www.museumca.org/goldrush

For a virtual tour of the Gold Rush exhibit at the Oakland Museum of California

Yahoo! Full Coverage: The Gold Rush

http://headlines.yahoo.com/Full_Coverage/Yahooligans/goldrush

For a comprehensive list of links to various sites related to the Gold Rush

Through the Mail

California Division of Tourism

801 K Street, Suite 1600

Sacramento, CA 95814

For information about visiting Gold Rush sites in California

On the Road

Marshall Gold Discovery State Historic Park

P.O. Box 265

310 Back Street

Coloma, CA 95613

530/622-3470

To see the gold discovery site

INDEX

American River, 5, 15

Baja peninsula, 14
Bear Flag, 14
Brannan, Sam, 7, *7*, 15

California Republic, 14
California Star (newspaper), *8*
California state constitution, 33
California state flower, 40
California state motto, 40
California state nickname, 40
California Trail, 10
Cape Horn, 10–11, *11*, *18*
cholera, 31
civil rights laws, 34
claims, 20–21, *21*
Clemens, Samuel, 24, *24*

denim, 31–32, *32*
disease, 30–31
Donner, George, 13
Donner, Jacob, 13
Donner Pass, *12*, 13

"Forty-Niners," 17, 40, *41*
Foster, Steven, 18
Frémont, John C., 13, 45

hard-rock mining, 26–27, *27*
Harte, Bret, 38, *38*
Levi's jeans, 32, *32*
lodes, 27
"The Luck of Roaring Camp"
    (Bret Harte), 38
lye, 6

Marshall, James, 5, *5*, 45
Mexican War, 13
miners, *15*, *19*, *23*, 24, *26*. *See also*
    prospectors.
mining towns, 22–23, *30*
Mother Lode, 27

Native Americans, 38–40
"The Notorious Jumping Frog of
    Calaveras County" (Mark
    Twain), 24

"Oh Susanna" (Stephen Foster),
    18
Oregon Trail, 10, 19
"The Outcasts of Poker Flat"
    (Bret Harte), 38

panning, 25, *25*, 28
peddlers, 28, *29*

Pleasant, Mary Ellen, 34, *34*, 45
pollution, 39
prospectors, 20. *See also* miners.

Reinhardt, Richard, 40
Sacramento Valley, 10
Sacramento Valley, California, 5
saloons, 24
"salted" claims, 21
San Francisco, California, 8, *36*,
    37–38
Sierra Nevada goldfield, 27
sluices, 26, *26*
Spain, 9, *9*
Stevens, Elisha, 10
Strauss, Levi, 31–32, 45
Sutter, John, 5, *5*, 45
Sutter's Mill, 15

transportation, *16*, 18–19, *19*
Twain, Mark. *See* Clemens,
    Samuel.

Yerba Buena, California, 37–38

women, 33–35, *35*

About the Author

Jean F. Blashfield has worked for publishers in Chicago, Illinois, and Washington, D.C. A graduate of the University of Michigan, she has written about ninety books, most of them for young people. Jean F. Blashfield has two college-age children and lives in Delavan, Wisconsin.